Titles in the series

British Library Cataloguing in Publication Data
Richardson, Joy, *1948-*
Eating.
1. Man. Eating. Regulation
I. Title   II. Series
613.2

ISBN 0-340-53256-4

First published 1991

Published by Hodder and Stoughton Children's Books,
a division of Hodder and Stoughton Ltd,
Mill Road, Dunton Green, Sevenoaks, Kent TN13 2YA

Printed in Italy

EATING

Joy Richardson

Illustrated by Polly Noakes

HODDER AND STOUGHTON
LONDON SYDNEY AUCKLAND TORONTO

Anna feels hungry. Her stomach is empty. 'Is breakfast ready?' she asks.

'May I have two slices of toast?'

2

Anna needs food to give her energy. People without food are like cars without fuel. They cannot keep going.

Anna munches her toast.

Watery saliva oozes out from
under her tongue and makes
the toast soggy.

Her tongue mixes it into a ball ready for swallowing.

The food goes down the food pipe in her neck and into her stomach. Anna does not feel hungry any more.

5

While Anna plays, her
stomach gets to work. The
stomach walls push and
squeeze the food, and mix it
up with stomach juices.

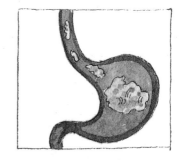

The food turns into
sloppy porridge.

After about an hour,
the food is ready to
leave her stomach.

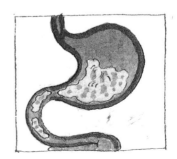

A hole opens at the end
and lets the food out a
little at a time.

The food travels on into her
intestines. Her intestines are
a long, long tube folded up
inside her.

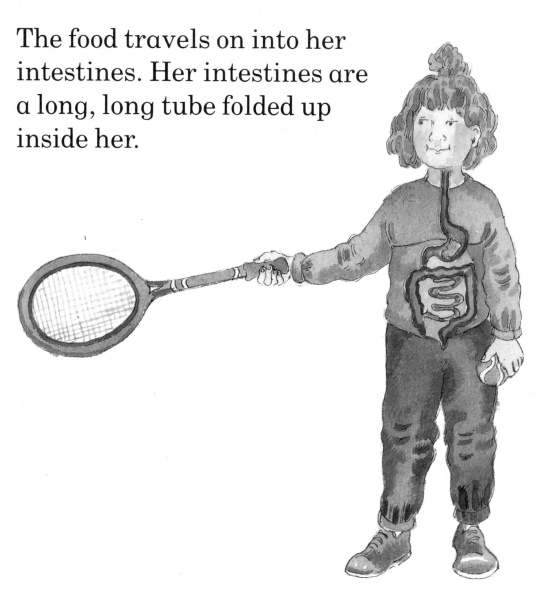

More juices make the food
very thin and watery.

In the walls of the intestines
there are tubes carrying blood.

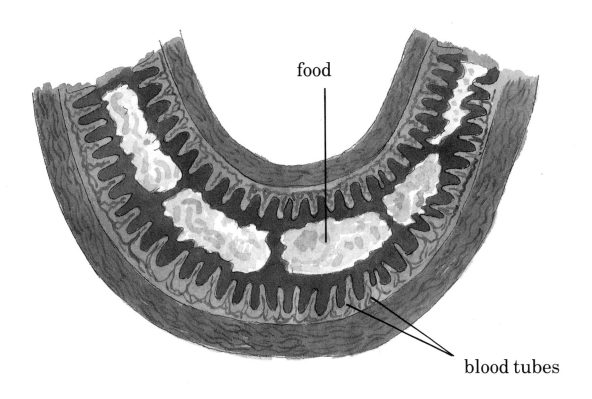

food

blood tubes

The watery food soaks through
the walls of the intestines into
the blood tubes.

9

Food which is not needed goes
on slowly to the end of the
intestines. It is quite solid now.
Anna pushes out the remains
when she goes to the lavatory.

The goodness from the food
mixes with the blood in the
walls of the intestines.

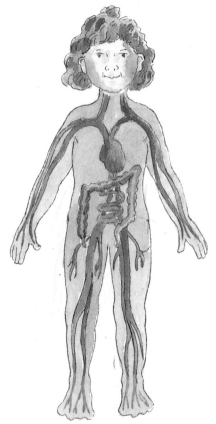

It travels quickly through
the blood tubes to every
part of the body.

Some of the food goes to the
muscles in Anna's body.

Anna runs across a field and
climbs over a gate. Food
makes the energy to move
her legs.

Anna lies on the grass. Her
heart goes on beating. She
never stops breathing.

Food makes the energy to keep
her insides working.

Some of the food is used for
growing. Anna's body is
made of what she eats. Food
builds new bits of body and
repairs old bits.

In just a few weeks Anna eats
as much as her body weighs.
Most of the food turns into
energy. Her body sorts out
what it needs for growing.

Anna watches the cows
eating grass.

Cows have four stomachs to
break up the grass and get out
all the goodness. Cows turn the
grass into milk and meat.

Cows chew and chew the grass
with big grinding teeth. Anna
has biting teeth at the front of
her mouth and chewing teeth
at the back.

Cows eat grass all the time.
Anna needs a mixture of
foods. Meat and milk help
her to grow. Bread gives her
energy.

Fruit and vegetables
keep her healthy.

'Yummy,' says Anna, 'this tastes good.' Her nose smells the food as she eats it. Little bumps on her tongue help to work out the tastes.

'Please may I have some sweets?' asks Anna.
'Not today,' says Mum.
Sweets taste nice but other foods are more use.

Anna eats over a thousand meals each year. Her body takes what it needs from the food she eats. Food keeps her going. Food keeps her growing.

Choose six foods. Blindfold a
friend. Put a little bit of one
food at a time on to a teaspoon.

Let your friend taste it. Can he
guess what it is?

Think of all the different foods
you have eaten today. How
many can you count?

eating words

food

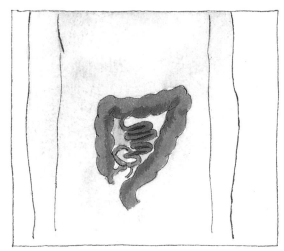

intestines

meal

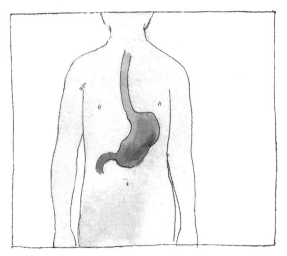

stomach

teeth

tongue